THE DINOSAUR LOVER'S COOKIE KIT

For Cookie Carnivores of All Ages

APPLESAUCE PRESS

Kennebunkport, Maine

INTRODUCTION

Sink Your Teeth into These Treats!

veryone loves cookies, and there's no limit to their different shapes and tastes! We collected dozens here for dinosaur lovers, big and small, with tons of gluten-free and dairy-free recipes, making them nom nom-able for all dinosaurs!

Note: not all of these cookies are to be cut out with your dinosaur-shaped cookie cutters, but they are still delicious and fun! Some would make great additions to a dinosaur-themed birthday party (more ideas later!) or they might help mommy and daddy dinosaurs get through the day! Try a whole herd to find your ferocious favorite, before they go extinct!

Now, gather the family and whip up some tasty treats!

BAKING BASICS

These are general pointers on procedures to be used for all genres of baked goods.

MEASURE ACCURATELY

✦ Measure dry ingredients in dry measuring cups, which are plastic or metal and come in sizes of ¼, ⅓, ½, and 1 cup. Spoon dry ingredients from the container or canister into the measuring cup, and then sweep the top with a straight edge such as the back of a knife or a spatula to measure it properly. Do not dip the cup into the canister or tap it on the counter to produce a level surface. These methods pack down the dry ingredients and can increase the actual volume by up to 10 percent. Tablespoons and teaspoons should also be leveled; a rounded ½ teaspoon can really measure almost 1 teaspoon. If the box or can does not have a straight edge built in, level the excess in the spoon back into the container with the back of a knife blade. Measure liquids in liquid measures, which come in different sizes but are transparent glass or plastic and have lines on the sides. To accurately measure liquids, place the measuring cup on a flat counter and bend down to read the marked level.

✦ Create consistent temperature. All ingredients should be at room temperature unless otherwise indicated. Having all ingredients at the same temperature makes it easier to combine them into a smooth, homogeneous mixture. Adding cold liquid to a dough or batter can cause the batter to lose its unified structure by making the fat rigid.

✦ Preheat the oven. Some ovens can take up to 25 minutes to reach a high temperature such as 450°F. The minimum heating time should be 15 minutes.

COOKIE-SPECIFIC TIPS

✦ Cool your cookie sheets by running the back under cold water between batches. Placing dough on a warm cookie sheet makes the cookies flatten.

✦ The last few cookies from a batch never seem to have as many "goodies," like chips or nuts as the first few cookies. Reserve some and mix them into the dough after about half of it has been scooped out for cookies. This way, the last of the cookies will have as much good stuff as the first batch.

- Take note of how far apart the mounds of cookie dough for drop cookies should be placed on the baking sheet. Some cookies spread far more than others.

- Rotate the cookie sheets midway through the baking time if using two sheets. Even if baking with a convection fan, cookies on an upper rack brown more quickly than those on a lower rack.

- Always allow cookies to cool for 2 minutes or as instructed in the individual recipe on the baking sheets before transferring them to cooling racks. Until they set up they are very fragile and can easily break apart on the spatula.

CANDY AND SPRINKLES

- The collection of colored and flavored sweets that can be affixed to cookies is almost endless. Some of them should be applied before the cookies are baked, and others need to be "glued" on with Raptor Royal Icing once cooled.

- As a general rule, any candy that can melt, like hard candies, miniature marshmallows, or jellybeans, should be applied after cooking, and any candy that is basically an ingredient, such as the coarse colored sugars, gold or silver dragées, nuts, or candied fruit, should be used before baking. Ingredients such as raisins can be used either way. If they are the "eyes" of gingerbread cavepeople or dinosaurs, it's probably best to place them before baking.

- A way to use colored sugars after cookies are baked is to create patterns with stencils. Spread either Raptor Royal Icing or Dino Dig-In Glaze (Confectioners' Sugar Glaze) on the cooled cookie, and then place a stencil made from parchment paper over it. Sprinkle sugars or sprinkles through the hole in the stencil.

PREHISTORIC PARTY TIPS

*Are you throwing a dino-mite
birthday party or sleepover?*

It's easy to host a dinosaur-themed party, and we've dug up some great tips and tricks for you and your paleontologists pals! Don't forget to send out invites to spread the word (just add –osuarus to the end of your name)!

SNACK-ASAURUS!

Set out some yummy snacks like chips and Dino Dip, or Protoceratops Pizza! Try to make a gigantic cookie for dessert, or a dinosaur-shaped cake! Sip Lava Juice or Swamp Juice! Here are some other ideas for snacks, depending on if you have a herd of plant-eaters or a pack of meat-eaters:

For the omnivores:

+ Chicken nuggets cut like dinosaurs (either with your cookie cutters or these can be found in the frozen food aisle, pre-cut)
+ Brachiosaurus Burgers (the more toppings, the better!)
+ T. rex Tacos
+ Hot lava dogs (Chili dogs, or the lava can be ketchup too!)

For the herbivores (vegetarians):

+ Pasta-Raptor Salad (pasta salad)
+ Dinosaur nest (shredded lettuce with cherry tomatoes or hard-boiled eggs on top)
+ Herbivore Salad (mixed greens with all kinds of veggies!)

FEROCIOUS FUN!

There are so many fun activities for a group of paleontologists, and if you go digging, keep your findings and discoveries for party favors!

+ Dig for dino bones (or candy) in an excavation! Be sure to bring a shovel and a headlamp!

- ✦ Hunt for dino eggs (like easter eggs) through a Jurassic jungle or desert, or try a dino egg on a spoon and race!

- ✦ Pin the tail on your favorite dino, like a diplodocus or an ankylosaurus!

- ✦ Catch your friends with Bronotosaurus, Bronotosaurus, T. REX! (This verison of "duck, duck, goose" is extra silly when you pretend to be a T. rex running!)

- ✦ Try pronouncing all of the dinosaur names in this book. Did you know that Micropachycephalosaurus is the hardest one to pronounce?! (Hint: it's MY-cro-PACK-ee-SEFF-ah-low-SORE-us)

Now you're geared up to have a *roaring-good time*!

DELICIOUS DINO COOKIE RECIPES

COOKIES

For All Cookie Carnivores!

SUGAR-SAURUS COOKIES
Sugar Cookies

YIELD: 2½ dozen • **ACTIVE TIME:** 20 minutes
START TO FINISH: 1½ hours, including 1 hour to chill dough

INGREDIENTS:

- ¾ cup butter
- 1 cup white sugar
- ½ teaspoon vanilla extract
- 2 eggs
- 2½ cups all-purpose flour
- 1 teaspoon baking powder
- ½ teaspoon salt

DIRECTIONS:

1. In a microwave-able bowl, soften the butter. Then blend in the sugar until combined thoroughly. Add in the vanilla extract and eggs and beat together.

2. Add flour, baking powder, and salt, stir together.

3. Cover the bowl and chill for about 1 hour or longer.

4. Before you take the dough out of the fridge, preheat oven to 400°F.

5. Flour your rolling surface (counter or cutting board), and roll out your chilled dough until it's about ¼- to ½-inch thick. Cut into the dough with your dinosaur cookie cutters!

6. On ungreased cookie sheets, set down the cookies, leaving about an inch of space between each.

7. Bake for 6 to 8 minutes in the oven. Let them cool entirely before decorating.

GINGER CAVEPEOPLE
Gingerbread People

YIELD: 3 dozen • **ACTIVE TIME:** 20 minutes
START TO FINISH: 30 minutes

INGREDIENTS:

- 7 cups all-purpose flour
- 2 teaspoons baking powder
- 2 teaspoons baking soda
- 1⅓ teaspoons ground ginger
- 2 teaspoons ground allspice
- 2 teaspoons ground cinnamon
- 2 teaspoon ground cloves
- 2 cups packed brown sugar
- 1 cup of butter, softened
- 1½ cup molasses
- 2 eggs, beaten

DIRECTIONS:

1. In a large bowl, combine 4 cups of your flour with baking soda and baking powder until all mixed together.

2. Add in the rest of the flour (3 cups) with the ginger, allspice, cinnamon, and cloves until evenly mixed. Add in the brown sugar.

3. Blend in the softened butter, molasses and eggs until thoroughly mixed. Cover the bowl and chill for 1 hour.

4. Preheat your oven to 350°F and flour your chosen rolling surface (cutting board or counter).

5. Roll out the dough until about ¼-inch thick, then use your dinosaur cookie cutters to create some ginger dinos or you may choose to make gingerbread cavemen (and women)!

6. Set the cut out shapes on a slightly greased cookie sheet, and space the cookies so they are 2 inches apart from each other.

7. Bake for 10 to 12 minutes in the oven. Let the cookies cool before decorating!

ALMOND-ALLOSAURUS
Spritz Cookies (Gluten-Free)

YIELD: 3-4 dozen • **ACTIVE TIME:** 20 minutes
START TO FINISH: 1½ hours, including 1 hour to chill dough

INGREDIENTS:

- 1 cup white rice flour
- 1 cup confectioners' sugar
- ½ cup sweet rice flour
- ½ cup potato starch
- ½ cup almond meal
- 1 teaspoon xanthan gum
- ½ pound (2 sticks) unsalted butter, sliced
- ¼ teaspoon salt
- 1 large egg
- 1 large egg white
- 1 teaspoon pure vanilla extract
- ½ teaspoon pure almond extract
- Gluten-free sugar sprinkles
- Small gluten-free candies

DIRECTIONS:

1. Combine white rice flour, confectioners' sugar, sweet rice flour, potato starch, almond meal, xanthan gum, and salt in a food processor fitted with the steel blade. Blend for 5 seconds. Add butter to the work bowl, and pulse until mixture resembles coarse meal.

2. Combine egg, egg white, vanilla, and almond extract in a small cup, and whisk well. Drizzle liquid into the work bowl, and pulse about 10 times, or until stiff dough forms. If dough is dry and doesn't come together, add milk by 1-teaspoon amounts, until dough forms a ball.

3. Divide dough in half, and wrap each half in plastic wrap. Press dough into a pancake. Refrigerate dough for 1 hour or until firm, or up to 2 days.

4. Preheat the oven to 350°F. Line two baking sheets with parchment paper or silicon baking mats.

5. Press dough through a cookie press onto the baking sheets. Decorate with sugar sprinkles and candies as desired.

6. Bake cookies for 10 to 12 minutes, or until edges are brown. Cool cookies for 2 minutes on the baking sheets, and then transfer them with a spatula to cooling racks to cool completely.

CHOMPING CHOCOLATE CHIP
Chocolate Chip Cookies

"I got this recipe off a bag of Gold Medal flour when I was a teenager, and it has stayed with me for many moves. It remains my go-to recipe for the best chocolate chip cookies ever. Thank you, Mary Bartz, who's credited with creating it, and to Gold Medal for making it widely available."

—Dominique DeVito

YIELD: 3½ dozen • **ACTIVE TIME:** 25 minutes
START TO FINISH: 45 minutes

INGREDIENTS:

- 1½ cups (3 sticks) butter or margarine, softened
- 1¼ cups granulated sugar
- 1¼ cups packed brown sugar
- 1 teaspoon vanilla extract
- 2 eggs
- 4 cups all-purpose flour
- 2 teaspoons baking soda
- 1 teaspoon salt
- 1 package (24 pounds, 4 cups) semisweet chocolate chips

DIRECTIONS:

1. Preheat the oven to 350°F.
2. In a large bowl, mix the butter, sugars, vanilla, and eggs. Stir in the flour, baking soda, and salt. Stir in the chocolate chips.
3. Drop dough by measuring rounded spoonfuls about 2 inches apart onto an ungreased cookie sheet.
4. Bake 12–15 minutes, or until light brown. Let cool slightly, remove from cookie sheet. Cool on wire rack.
5. Bake for 10 to 12 minutes in the oven. Let the cookies cool before decorating!

PRESERVED AMBER COOKIES
Linzer Cookies (Gluten-Free)

YIELD: 2 dozen • **ACTIVE TIME:** 30 minutes
START TO FINISH: 1¾ hours, including one hour to chill dough

INGREDIENTS:

- 1½ cups white rice flour
- ¾ cup almond meal
- 1¼ teaspoons xanthan gum
- ½ teaspoon salt
- ¼ pound (1 stick) soft unsalted butter
- ¾ teaspoons gluten-free baking powder

- ¾ cup granulated sugar
- 1 large egg
- 1 tablespoon whole milk
- ¾ teaspoon pure almond extract
- Sweet rice flour
- ¾ cup seedless raspberry jam
- ⅓ cup confectioners' sugar

DIRECTIONS:

1. Combine rice flour, almond meal, xanthan gum, baking powder, and salt in a mixing bowl. Whisk well. Combine butter and sugar in another mixing bowl and beat at low speed with an electric mixer. Increase the speed to high, and beat for 3 to 4 minutes, or until light and fluffy. Add egg, milk, and almond extract, and beat for 1 minute.

2. Slowly add dry ingredients to the butter mixture, and beat until stiff dough forms. Wrap dough in plastic wrap. Press dough into a pancake. Refrigerate dough for 1 hour or until firm, or up to 2 days.

3. Preheat the oven to 350°F. Line two baking sheets with parchment paper or silicon baking mats.

4. Lightly dust a sheet of waxed paper and a rolling pin with sweet rice flour. Roll dough to a thickness of ⅛ inch. Dip a 2-inch flower-shaped cookie cutter in sweet rice flour, and cut out 48 cookies. Remove excess dough, and transfer cookies to the baking sheets. Cut holes with a ¾-inch cutter in the center of 24 cookies. Re-roll excess dough, chilling it for 15 minutes if necessary.

5. Bake cookies for 8 to 10 minutes, or until edges are brown. Cool cookies for 2 minutes on the baking sheets, and then transfer them with a spatula to cooling racks to cool completely.

6. Spread jam on the 24 cookies without the holes. Dust remaining cookies with confectioners' sugar. Place cookies with holes on top of the jam-covered cookies.

VOLCANIC CRUST CRACKERS
Graham Crackers (Gluten-Free)

YIELD: 16-20, depending on size • **ACTIVE TIME:** 20 minutes
START TO FINISH: 1¾ hours, including 1 hour to chill dough

INGREDIENTS:

- 1½ cups brown rice flour
- ½ cup cornstarch
- ⅓ cup firmly packed dark brown sugar
- 1 teaspoon baking powder
- ¾ teaspoon xanthan gum
- ½ teaspoon ground cinnamon
- ½ teaspoon salt
- 6 tablespoons (¾ stick) unsalted butter, sliced
- 5 tablespoons whole milk
- ¼ cup honey
- ½ teaspoon pure vanilla extract
- Sweet rice flour

DIRECTIONS:

1. Combine rice flour, cornstarch, sugar, baking powder, xanthan gum, cinnamon, and salt in a food processor fitted with the steel blade. Blend for 5 seconds. Add butter to the work bowl, and process, using on-and-off pulsing, until mixture resembles coarse meal.

2. Combine milk, honey, and vanilla in a small cup, and whisk well. Drizzle liquid into the work bowl, and pulse about 10 times, or until stiff dough forms. If dough is dry and doesn't come together add additional milk by 1-teaspoon amounts, until dough forms a ball.

3. Divide dough in half, and wrap each half in plastic wrap. Press dough into a pancake. Refrigerate dough for 1 hour or until firm, or up to 2 days.

4. Preheat the oven to 350°F. Line two baking sheets with parchment paper or silicon baking mats.

5. Lightly dust a sheet of waxed paper and a rolling pin with sweet rice flour. Roll each half of dough into a rectangle ¼-inch thick. Transfer dough to the prepared baking sheets, and cut each half into 8 to 10 rectangles with a pizza wheel. Prick dough all over with the tines of a fork.

6. Bake cookies for 15 to 17 minutes, or until browned. Allow cookies to cool completely on the cookie sheets placed on a wire cooling rack.

VARIATION: *Sprinkle cookies with a mixture of ⅓ cup granulated sugar and 1 teaspoon ground cinnamon before baking.*

SWAMP SQUARES
Lemon Squares (Gluten-Free)

YIELD: 2-3 dozen • **ACTIVE TIME:** 15 minutes
START TO FINISH: 1 hours

INGREDIENTS:

+ ¼ cup brown rice flour
+ ¼ cup confectioners' sugar
+ ¼ cup sweet rice flour
+ ¼ cup potato starch
+ ¼ cup almond meal
+ ½ teaspoon xanthan gum
+ ¼ teaspoon salt
+ 3 large eggs, divided

+ ¼ pound (1 stick) unsalted butter, sliced
+ ½ teaspoon pure vanilla extract
+ 1 cup granulated sugar
+ 1 tablespoon cornstarch
+ ⅓ cup freshly squeezed lemon juice
+ 1 tablespoon grated lemon zest
+ Confectioners' sugar for dusting

DIRECTIONS:

1. Preheat the oven to 350°F. Line a 9 x 9-inch baking pan with heavy-duty aluminum foil, allowing the sides to be long and wrapped around the sides of the pan. Grease the foil.

2. Combine rice flour, confectioners' sugar, sweet rice flour, potato starch, almond meal, xanthan gum, and salt in a food processor fitted with the steel blade. Blend for 5 seconds. Add butter to the work bowl, and process, using on-and-off pulsing, until mixture resembles coarse meal.

3. Combine 1 egg and vanilla in a small cup, and whisk well. Drizzle liquid into the work bowl, and pulse about 10 times, or until stiff dough forms. If dough is dry and doesn't come together add milk by 1 teaspoon amounts, until dough forms a ball. Press dough into the bottom of the prepared pan. Bake crust for 20 minutes, or until lightly browned.

4. While crust bakes, prepare topping. Combine remaining 2 eggs, sugar, cornstarch, lemon juice, and lemon zest in a mixing bowl. Beat at medium speed with an electric mixer for 1 minute, or until well blended.

5. Pour topping over crust and bake for 20 minutes, or until barely brown. Custard should still be soft. Dust with confectioners' sugar. Cool completely in the pan on a cooling rack, then cut into pieces.

   Note: The cookies can be refrigerated for up to 1 week, tightly covered.

JURASSIC JELLY AND PEANUT BUTTER BARS

Peanut Butter and Jelly Bars (Vegan)

YIELD: 1½ dozen • **ACTIVE TIME:** 15 minutes
START TO FINISH: 40 minutes

INGREDIENTS:

- ✦ 1½ teaspoons egg replacement powder, such as Ener-G
- ✦ ¾ cup packed light brown sugar
- ✦ ½ cup (8 tablespoons) soft soy margarine
- ✦ ¾ cup commercial chunky peanut butter
- ✦ 1 cup seedless raspberry jam
- ✦ ½ teaspoon pure vanilla extract
- ✦ ½ teaspoon baking powder
- ✦ ¼ teaspoon salt
- ✦ 1½ cups whole-wheat pastry flour
- ✦ ¾ cup chopped roasted peanuts

DIRECTIONS:

1. Preheat the oven to 350°F. Line the bottom and sides of an 8 x 8-inch baking pan with parchment paper or foil, allowing the paper to extend 2 inches over the top of the pan. Grease the paper.

2. Combine egg replacement powder and 2 tablespoons cold water, and set aside. Place jam in a saucepan and bring to a boil over medium heat, stirring frequently. Reduce the heat to low and simmer jam until reduced by one-fourth. Set aside.

3. Combine margarine, peanut butter, and sugar in a mixing bowl, and beat at low speed with an electric mixer to blend. Increase the speed to high, and beat for 3 to 4 minutes, or until light and fluffy. Beat in egg replacement mixture, vanilla, baking powder, and salt and beat for 1 minute. Slowly add flour to margarine mixture, and beat until soft dough forms. Stir in peanuts.

4. Pat ⅔ of dough into the bottom of the prepared pan. Make dollops with jam, and spread evenly over crust. Break remaining dough into 1-tablespoon pieces, flatten between your hands, and arrange on top of jam.

5. Bake bars for 25 to 30 minutes, or until top is golden brown. Cool completely on a wire rack. Lift up the ends of the parchment or foil liner, transfer brownies to a cutting board, and cut into pieces.

Note: The brownies can be made up to 3 days in advance and kept at room temperature in an airtight container.

PREHISTORIC PEANUT BUTTER
Peanut Butter Cookies (Gluten-Free)

YIELD: 2-3 dozen • **ACTIVE TIME:** 20 minutes
START TO FINISH: 35 minutes

INGREDIENTS:

- 1 cup brown rice flour
- ¼ cup tapioca flour
- ¼ cup cornstarch
- 1¼ teaspoons gluten-free baking powder
- ½ teaspoon xanthan gum
- ½ teaspoon salt
- 1 stick unsalted butter, softened
- 1 cup peanut butter (either smooth or chunky)
- ½ cup granulated sugar
- ½ cup packed dark brown sugar
- 1 large egg
- 1 large egg yolk
- ½ teaspoon pure vanilla extract

DIRECTIONS:

1. Preheat the oven to 375°F. Line two baking sheets with parchment paper or silicon baking mats.

2. Combine rice flour, tapioca flour, cornstarch, baking powder, xanthan gum, and salt in a mixing bowl. Whisk well.

3. Combine butter, peanut butter, granulated sugar, and brown sugar in another mixing bowl and beat at low speed with an electric mixer to combine. Increase the speed to high, and beat for 3 to 4 minutes, or until light and fluffy. Add egg, egg yolk, and vanilla, and beat for 1 minute.

4. Slowly add dry ingredients to the butter mixture, and beat until stiff dough forms.

5. Form 1-tablespoon amounts of dough into balls, and transfer balls to the prepared baking sheets, leaving 2 inches of space between balls. Flatten balls with the tines of a fork to make a crosshatch pattern.

6. Bake for 8 to 10 minutes, or until golden brown. Cool cookies on the baking sheets for 2 minutes, and then transfer to a wire rack to cool completely.

VARIATION: *Add 1 cup chocolate chips to the dough before baking.*

DINO DOODLES
Snickerdoodles (Vegan)

YIELD: 2½ dozen • **ACTIVE TIME:** 15 minutes
START TO FINISH: 40 minutes

INGREDIENTS:

- 1 cups granulated sugar, divided
- 2 tablespoons soy milk
- 1 teaspoon pure vanilla extract
- 1 cup all-purpose flour
- ⅔ cup whole-wheat pastry flour
- 2 tablespoons cornstarch
- 1 teaspoon baking powder
- 1 cup (16 tablespoons) soft soy margarine
- ¼ teaspoon salt
- 1 teaspoon ground cinnamon
- ¼ teaspoon freshly grated nutmeg

DIRECTIONS:

1. Preheat the oven to 350°F. Line two baking sheets with parchment paper or silicone baking mats.

2. Combine margarine, 1¼ cups sugar, soy milk, and vanilla in a mixing bowl, and beat at low speed with an electric mixer to blend. Increase the speed to high, and beat for 3 to 4 minutes, or until light and fluffy. Reduce the speed to low and add all-purpose and whole-wheat flours, cornstarch, baking powder, and salt until just blended in.

3. Combine remaining sugar, cinnamon, and nutmeg in a small bowl. Take scant 1-tablespoon portions of dough, and roll them into balls. Roll balls in sugar mixture. Arrange balls 2 inches apart on the prepared baking sheets.

4. Bake for 12 to 14 minutes, or until lightly brown around the edges. Cool for 2 minutes on the baking sheets, and then transfer cookies to racks to cool completely.

Note: Keep cookies in an airtight container, layered between sheets of waxed paper or parchment, at room temperature for up to 5 days. Cookies can also be frozen for up to 2 months.

FOSSILIZED FAVORITES
Chocolate Chip Oatmeal Cookies (Vegan)

YIELD: 3 dozen • **ACTIVE TIME:** 15 minutes
START TO FINISH: 30 minutes

INGREDIENTS:

+ ½ cup (8 tablespoons) soft soy margarine
+ ½ cup firmly packed light brown sugar
+ ½ cup granulated sugar
+ ½ cup peanut oil
+ 1 (12 ounce) package [vegan] semi-sweet chocolate chips, or more, to taste
+ ¼ cup mashed ripe banana
+ 1 teaspoon pure vanilla extract
+ 1 cup all-purpose flour
+ ¾ cup whole-wheat pastry flour
+ 1½ teaspoons baking powder
+ ¼ teaspoon salt
+ 1 cup quick oats

DIRECTIONS:

1. Preheat oven to 350°F. Line two baking sheets with parchment paper or silicone baking mats.

2. Combine margarine, brown sugar, and granulated sugar in a mixing bowl, and beat at low speed with an electric mixer to blend. Increase the speed to high, and beat for 3 to 4 minutes, or until light and fluffy. Add oil, banana, and vanilla, and beat for 1 minute. Reduce the speed to low and add all-purpose and whole-wheat flours, baking powder, and salt until just blended in. Stir in oats and chocolate chips.

3. Drop batter by tablespoons onto the baking sheets, spacing them 2 inches apart. Bake for 12 to 15 minutes, or until edges are brown. Cool for 2 minutes on the baking sheets, and then transfer cookies to racks to cool completely.

   Note: Keep cookies in an airtight container, layered between sheets of waxed paper or parchment, at room temperature for up to 5 days. Cookies can also be frozen for up to 2 months.

VARIATION: Substitute raisins, or chopped, candied or dried fruit for the chocolate chips.

MESOZOIC CHOCOLATE COOKIES

Mexican Chocolate Cookies (Gluten-Free)

YIELD: 2 dozen • **ACTIVE TIME:** 20 minutes
START TO FINISH: 40 minutes

INGREDIENTS:

- 1½ cups blanched almonds
- 3 cups confectioners' sugar, divided
- ½ teaspoon salt
- 1 teaspoon ground cinnamon
- ½ teaspoon pure almond extract
- ¾ cup Dutch-process cocoa powder
- 4 large egg whites, at room temperature
- 5 ounces bittersweet chocolate, chopped

DIRECTIONS:

1. Preheat oven to 350°F. Line two baking sheets with parchment paper or silicon baking mats. Place almonds on a baking sheet, and toast for 5 to 7 minutes, or until lightly browned.

2. Decrease the oven temperature to 325°F. Place almonds and 1 cup sugar in a food processor fitted with the steel blade, and chop almonds finely using on-and-off pulsing.

3. Scrape almond mixture into a mixing bowl, and add remaining sugar, cocoa powder, cinnamon, and salt. Whisk well, and stir in chocolate, egg whites, and almond extract. Stir well.

4. Drop dough by heaping 1-tablespoon portions onto the prepared baking sheets, 2 inches apart. Bake cookies for 20 to 25 minutes, or until cookies are dry. Cool cookies for 2 minutes on the baking sheets, and then transfer to a wire rack to cool completely.

FROZEN FOSSILS

Snowball or Mexican Wedding Cookies (Gluten-Free)

YIELD: 3 dozen • **ACTIVE TIME:** 15 minutes
START TO FINISH: 30 minutes

INGREDIENTS:

- 1 cup chopped pecans
- 1½ cups white rice flour
- ¼ cup potato starch
- ¼ cup sweet rice flour
- ½ teaspoon xanthan gum
- ½ teaspoon salt
- ½ pound (2 sticks) unsalted butter
- 1 teaspoon pure vanilla extract
- 1½ cups confectioners' sugar, divided

DIRECTIONS:

1. Preheat the oven to 350°F. Line two baking sheets with parchment paper or silicon baking mats. Place pecans on a baking sheet, and toast for 5 to 7 minutes, or until lightly browned. Set aside. Reduce the oven temperature to 325°F.

2. Combine rice flour, potato starch, sweet rice flour, xanthan gum, and salt in a mixing bowl. Whisk well.

3. Combine butter and 1 cup sugar in another mixing bowl and beat at low speed with an electric mixer to combine. Increase the speed to high, and beat for 3 to 4 minutes, or until light and fluffy. Add vanilla, and beat for 1 minute.

4. Slowly add dry ingredients to the butter mixture, and beat until stiff dough forms. Fold in pecans.

5. Form dough into 1-tablespoon mounds on the baking sheets, 1½ inches apart. Bake cookies for 15 to 20 minutes, or until lightly brown. Cool for 2 minutes on the baking sheets.

6. Place remaining ½ cup confectioners' sugar in a shallow bowl. Dip tops of cookies in sugar, and then cool completely on a cooling rack.

HERBIVORE TEETH
Ginger Shortbread Fingers (Gluten-Free)

YIELD: 2 dozen • **ACTIVE TIME:** 25 minutes
START TO FINISH: 1¾ hours, including 1 hour to chill dough

INGREDIENTS:

- ½ pound (2 sticks) soft unsalted butter
- 2 cups brown rice flour
- ⅓ cup sweet rice flour
- ⅓ cup almond meal
- ⅔ cup firmly packed light brown sugar
- 1 teaspoon xanthan gum
- ½ teaspoon salt
- ½ cup very finely chopped crystallized ginger
- ½ teaspoon pure vanilla extract
- Sweet rice flour

DIRECTIONS:

1. Combine rice flour, sweet rice flour, almond meal, xanthan gum, and salt in a mixing bowl. Whisk well.

2. Combine butter and sugar in another mixing bowl and beat at low speed with an electric mixer to combine. Increase the speed to high, and beat for 3 to 4 minutes, or until light and fluffy. Add crystallized ginger and vanilla, and beat for 1 minute.

3. Slowly add dry ingredients to butter mixture, and beat until stiff dough forms. Wrap dough in plastic wrap. Press dough into a pancake. Refrigerate dough for 1 hour or until firm, or up to 2 days.

4. Preheat the oven to 350°F. Line two baking sheets with parchment paper or silicon baking mats.

5. Lightly dust a sheet of waxed paper and a rolling pin with sweet rice flour. Roll dough to a thickness of ½-inch. Cut into rectangles 4 inches long and 1-inch wide. Transfer cookies to the baking sheets. Re-roll excess dough, chilling it for 15 minutes if necessary.

6. Bake cookies for 12 to 15 minutes, or until edges are brown. Cool cookies for 2 minutes on the baking sheets, and then transfer them with a spatula to cooling racks to cool completely.

VARIATION: *Dip one end of cooled cookies into melted white chocolate, and sprinkle with colored sugars.*

MOMMY DINO'S PICK ME UP
Coffee Ginger Shortbread Slivers (Vegan)

For full-grown dinosaur lovers only!

YIELD: 2 dozen • **ACTIVE TIME:** 15 minutes
START TO FINISH: 45 minutes

INGREDIENTS:

- 3 tablespoons granulated sugar
- ½ cup whole-wheat pastry flour
- 1 tablespoon instant espresso powder
- 1 cup (16 tablespoons) soft soy margarine
- 1½ teaspoons ground ginger
- ½ teaspoon ground cinnamon
- 2 cups all-purpose flour
- ¾ cup firmly packed light brown sugar
- ½ cup finely chopped crystallized ginger
- ¼ teaspoon salt

DIRECTIONS:

1. Preheat the oven to 350°F, and grease two (10-inch) pie plates. Combine espresso powder with 2 tablespoons boiling water, and stir well. Set aside.

2. Combine margarine and sugar in a mixing bowl, and beat at low speed with an electric mixer until blended. Increase the speed to high, and beat for 3 to 4 minutes, or until light and fluffy. Reduce the speed to low, and add coffee mixture, ginger, cinnamon, salt, and the all-purpose and pastry flours.

3. Press dough into the prepared pie plates, extending the sides up ½-inch. Pat on crystallized ginger and sprinkle with granulated sugar evenly. Cut dough into 12 thin wedges. Prick surface of dough all over with the tines of a fork.

4. Bake for 30 minutes, or until dough is lightly browned at the edges. Remove the pans from the oven, and go over cut lines again. Cool completely in the pans on a wire rack, and then remove slivers from the pie plates with a small spatula.

Note: Keep cookies in an airtight container, layered between sheets of waxed paper or parchment, at room temperature for up to 5 days. Cookies can also be frozen for up to 2 months.

PEPPERMINT PARKSOSAURUS CHOCOLATE CLAWS

Chocolate Peppermint Biscotti (Gluten-Free)

YIELD: 2 dozen • **ACTIVE TIME:** 25 minutes
START TO FINISH: 2 hours

INGREDIENTS:

- 1 cup brown rice flour
- ⅓ cup potato starch
- 3 tablespoons tapioca starch
- 1 teaspoon xanthan gum
- 1¼ pound (1 stick) soft unsalted butter
- ¼ teaspoon salt
- ½ cup unsweetened cocoa powder
- 2½ cups confectioners' sugar divided
- ½ teaspoon gluten-free baking powder
- 2 large eggs
- 1 (3 ounces) package softened cream cheese
- ½ cup crushed peppermint candies
- ¾ teaspoon peppermint oil or pure peppermint extract, divided

DIRECTIONS:

1. Preheat the oven to 350°F. Line a baking sheet with parchment paper or a silicon baking mat.

2. Combine rice flour, cocoa, potato starch, tapioca starch, xanthan gum, baking powder, and salt in a mixing bowl. Whisk well. Combine butter and 1¼ cups sugar in another mixing bowl and beat at low speed with an electric mixer to combine. Increase the speed to high, and beat for 3 to 4 minutes, or until light and fluffy. Add eggs and ½ teaspoon peppermint oil, and beat for 1 minute.

3. Slowly add dry ingredients to the butter mixture, and beat until stiff dough forms. Form dough into a log 12 inches long and 3 inches wide on the prepared baking sheet. Bake until light golden, about 40 minutes. Cool for 30 minutes.

4. Place log on a cutting board. Cut log on a diagonal into ½- to ¾ -inch-thick slices using a sharp, serrated knife. Arrange biscotti, cut side down, on the baking sheet. Bake for 15 minutes, or until pale golden. Transfer biscotti to a rack and cool completely.

5. For frosting, combine cream cheese, remaining sugar, and remaining peppermint oil in a mixing bowl. Beat at low speed with an electric mixer to combine. Increase the speed to high, and beat for 2 to 3 minutes, or until light and fluffy. Spread frosting on top of thin edge of cookies, and pat peppermint candies on top.

TEN-TON TALONS
Almond Biscotti (Gluten-Free)

YIELD: 2 dozen • **ACTIVE TIME:** 20 minutes
START TO FINISH: 1¾ hours

INGREDIENTS:

- 1½ cups sliced almonds
- ½ cup brown rice flour
- ½ teaspoon gluten-free baking powder
- ½ cup almond meal
- ⅓ cup potato starch
- 3 tablespoons tapioca starch

- 1 teaspoon xanthan gum
- ¼ teaspoon salt
- ¼ pound (1 stick) unsalted butter, softened
- 1¼ cups confectioners' sugar
- 2 large eggs
- 1 teaspoon pure almond extract

DIRECTIONS:

1. Preheat the oven to 350°F. Line a baking sheet with parchment paper or a silicon baking mat.

2. Place almonds on a baking sheet, and toast for 5 to 7 minutes, or until lightly browned. Remove nuts from the oven, and set aside.

3. Combine rice flour, almond meal, potato starch, tapioca starch, xanthan gum, baking powder, and salt in a mixing bowl. Whisk well.

4. Combine butter and confectioners' sugar in another mixing bowl and beat at low speed with an electric mixer to combine. Increase the speed to high, and beat for 3 to 4 minutes, or until light and fluffy. Add eggs and almond extract, and beat for 1 minute.

5. Slowly add dry ingredients to the butter mixture, and beat until stiff dough forms. Fold almonds into dough.

6. Form dough into a log 12 inches long and 3 inches wide on the prepared baking sheet. Bake until light golden, about 40 minutes. Cool for 30 minutes.

7. Place log on a cutting board. Cut log on a diagonal into ½- to ¾ -inch-thick slices using a sharp, serrated knife. Arrange biscotti, cut side down, on the baking sheet. Bake for 15 minutes, or until pale golden. Transfer biscotti to a rack and cool completely.

   Note: If you want soft biscotti rather than hard ones, don't bake them a second time. Bake them for 45 minutes, and then let the log cool for 5 minutes before slicing.

CARNIVORE CLUSTERS
Granola Cookies (Vegan)

YIELD: 4 dozen • **ACTIVE TIME:** 25 minutes
START TO FINISH: 1¾ hours, including 1 hour to chill dough

INGREDIENTS:

- 2 cups brown rice flour
- ⅓ cup sweet rice flour
- ⅓ cup almond meal
- 1 teaspoon xanthan gum
- ½ teaspoon salt
- 2 sticks unsalted butter, softened
- ⅔ cup firmly packed light brown sugar
- ½ cup very finely chopped crystallized ginger
- ½ teaspoon pure vanilla extract
- Sweet rice flour

DIRECTIONS:

1. Combine rice flour, sweet rice flour, almond meal, xanthan gum, and salt in a mixing bowl. Whisk well.

2. Combine butter and sugar in another mixing bowl and beat at low speed with an electric mixer to combine. Increase the speed to high, and beat for 3 to 4 minutes, or until light and fluffy. Add crystallized ginger and vanilla, and beat for 1 minute.

3. Slowly add dry ingredients to butter mixture, and beat until stiff dough forms. Wrap dough in plastic wrap. Press dough into a pancake. Refrigerate dough for 1 hour or until firm, or up to 2 days.

4. Preheat the oven to 350°F. Line two baking sheets with parchment paper or silicon baking mats.

5. Lightly dust a sheet of waxed paper and a rolling pin with sweet rice flour. Roll dough to a thickness of ½-inch. Cut into rectangles 4 inches long and 1-inch wide. Transfer cookies to the baking sheets. Re-roll excess dough, chilling it for 15 minutes if necessary.

6. Bake cookies for 12 to 15 minutes, or until edges are brown. Cool cookies for 2 minutes on the baking sheets, and then transfer them with a spatula to cooling racks to cool completely.

VARIATION: Dip one end of cooled cookies into melted white chocolate, and sprinkle with colored sugars.

OMNIVORE OATMEAL
Oatmeal Cookies (Vegan)

YIELD: 3-4 dozen • **ACTIVE TIME:** 15 minutes
START TO FINISH: 30 minutes

INGREDIENTS:

+ 1 tablespoon egg replacement powder, such as Ener-G
+ ⅓ cup (6 tablespoons) soy margarine, softened
+ ½ cup granulated sugar
+ ½ cup firmly packed dark brown sugar
+ 1 teaspoon pure vanilla extract
+ 1 teaspoon ground cinnamon
+ ½ teaspoon baking soda
+ Pinch of salt
+ 1 cup all-purpose flour
+ 1¼ cups quick-cooking or old-fashioned oats (not instant)
+ 1 cup dried cranberries, raisins or apricots
+ 1 cup chopped pistachio nuts

DIRECTIONS:

1. Preheat the oven to 375°F. Line two baking sheets with parchment paper or silicone baking mats.

2. Mix egg replacement powder with ¼ cup cold water, and set aside. Combine margarine, granulated sugar, and brown sugar in a mixing bowl, and beat at low speed with an electric mixer to blend. Increase the speed to high, and beat for 3 to 4 minutes, or until light and fluffy. Add egg replacement mixture, vanilla, cinnamon, baking soda, and salt, and beat for 2 minutes more. Reduce the speed to low and add flour until just blended in. Stir in oats, cranberries, and pistachios.

3. Drop batter by tablespoons onto the baking sheets, spacing them 2 inches apart. Bake for 12 to 15 minutes, or until edges are brown. Cool for 2 minutes on the baking sheets, and then transfer cookies to racks to cool completely.

Note: Keep cookies in an airtight container, layered between sheets of waxed paper or parchment, at room temperature for up to 5 days. Cookies can also be frozen for up to 2 months.

BRONTORNIS NEST

Crunchy Peanut Butter and Cherry Thumbprints (Vegan)

YIELD: 3 dozen • **ACTIVE TIME:** 20 minutes
START TO FINISH: 45 minutes

INGREDIENTS:

- ✦ 1½ teaspoons egg replacement powder, such as Ener-G
- ✦ ½ teaspoon pure vanilla extract
- ✦ 1 teaspoon baking soda
- ✦ ½ cup (8 tablespoons) soy margarine, softened
- ✦ 1 cup smooth commercial peanut butter (not homemade or natural)
- ✦ ¾ cup firmly packed light brown sugar
- ✦ ¼ teaspoon salt
- ✦ 1 cup all-purpose flour
- ✦ 1 cup finely chopped roasted peanuts (not dry-roasted)
- ✦ 18 candied cherries, halved, in whatever color you prefer!

DIRECTIONS:

1. Preheat the oven to 375°F. Line two baking sheets with parchment paper or silicone baking mats.

2. Mix egg replacement powder with 2 tablespoons cold water, and set aside. Combine sugar, margarine, and peanut butter in a mixing bowl, and beat at low speed with an electric mixer to blend. Increase the speed to high, and beat for 3 to 4 minutes, or until light and fluffy. Beat in egg replacement mixture, vanilla, baking soda, and salt and beat for 1 minute. Slowly add flour to margarine mixture, and beat until soft dough forms.

3. Take scant 1-tablespoon portions of dough, and roll them into balls. Roll balls in chopped peanuts. Place balls 1½ inches apart on the baking sheets, and make a shallow depression with your index finger in the center of each ball. Insert 1 cherry half into each depression.

4. Bake cookies for 10 to 12 minutes, or until edges are brown. Cool cookies for 2 minutes on baking sheets, then transfer cookies to racks to cool completely.

   Note: Keep cookies in an airtight container, layered between sheets of waxed paper or parchment, at room temperature for up to 5 days.

VARIATION: *Substitute a few chocolate chips for the cherries, and place them on the cookies prior to baking.*

SCORCHED EARTH
Chocolate Crackles (Vegan)

YIELD: 3 dozen • **ACTIVE TIME:** 20 minutes
START TO FINISH: 45 minutes

INGREDIENTS:

- 2 cups confectioners' sugar, divided
- ¼ cup silken tofu
- ½ teaspoon pure vanilla extract
- ⅓ cup unsweetened cocoa powder
- 2 tablespoons cold water
- ⅔ cup all-purpose flour
- ⅔ cup whole-wheat pastry flour
- Pinch of salt
- ½ cup (8 tablespoons) soy margarine, softened

DIRECTIONS:

1. Preheat the oven to 350°F. Line two baking sheets with parchment paper or silicone baking mats.

2. Combine margarine and ½ cup sugar in a mixing bowl, and beat at medium speed with an electric mixer until light and fluffy. Add tofu and vanilla, and beat well. Add cocoa powder, and beat well, scraping the sides of the bowl as necessary. Reduce the speed to low, and add all-purpose and whole-wheat flours, and salt. Beat until just combined.

3. Form dough into 1-inch balls, and place them 1 inch apart on the prepared baking sheets. Bake for 15 to 18 minutes, or until firm. Sift remaining confectioners' sugar into a low bowl, and add a few cookies at a time, rolling them around in the sugar to coat them well. Transfer cookies to racks to cool completely.

Note: Keep cookies in an airtight container, layered between sheets of waxed paper or parchment, at room temperature for up to 5 days. Cookies can also be frozen for up to 2 months.

TRICERATOPS TEA COOKIES
Lemon-Glazed Tea Shortbread Slivers (Vegan)

For the most distinguished of dinosaurs!

YIELD: 2 dozen • **ACTIVE TIME:** 15 minutes
START TO FINISH: 45 minutes

INGREDIENTS:

- ✦ 2 tablespoons Earl Grey tea leaves
- ✦ 1½ cups granulated sugar, divided
- ✦ 1 cup (16 tablespoons) soy margarine, softened
- ✦ ½ teaspoon pure vanilla extract
- ✦ 2 cups all-purpose flour
- ✦ ½ cup cornstarch
- ✦ ¼ teaspoon salt
- ✦ 1½ cups confectioners' sugar
- ✦ 1 tablespoon grated lemon zest
- ✦ 3 tablespoons freshly squeezed lemon juice

DIRECTIONS:

1. Preheat the oven to 350°F, and grease two (10-inch) pie plates.

2. Combine tea leaves and ½ cup sugar in a food processor fitted with the steel blade or in a blender. Process until smooth, and transfer mixture to a mixing bowl. Add remaining sugar, margarine, and vanilla, and beat at low speed with an electric mixer until blended. Increase the speed to high, and beat for 3 to 4 minutes, or until light and fluffy. Reduce the speed to low, and add flour, cornstarch, and salt. Beat until well blended.

3. Press dough into the prepared pie plates, extending the sides up ½ inch. Cut dough into 12 thin wedges. Prick surface of dough all over with the tines of a fork.

4. Bake for 30 minutes, or until dough is lightly browned at the edges. Remove the pans from the oven, and go over cut lines again. Cool completely in the pans on a wire rack.

5. Combine confectioners' sugar, lemon zest, and lemon juice in a bowl. Whisk well. Spread glaze over shortbreads, and allow to set for 15 minutes. Remove slivers from the pie plates with a small spatula.

Note: Keep cookies in an airtight container, layered between sheets of waxed paper or parchment, at room temperature for up to 5 days. Cookies can also be frozen for up to 2 months.

BRONTOSAURUS BARS
Almond Bars (Gluten-Free)

YIELD: 2-3 dozen • **ACTIVE TIME:** 15 minutes
START TO FINISH: 1 hour

INGREDIENTS:

- ¾ cup brown rice flour
- ¾ cup confectioners' sugar
- ½ cup potato starch
- ½ teaspoon xanthan gum
- ½ teaspoon baking soda
- ½ teaspoon salt
- ⅓ cup firmly packed almond paste

- 1 large egg
- 1 tablespoon whole milk
- 1 teaspoon pure almond extract
- 1 large egg white
- 1 cup sliced almonds
- 12 tablespoons (1½ sticks) unsalted butter, sliced

DIRECTIONS:

1. Preheat the oven to 350°F. Grease a 9 x 9-inch baking pan.

2. Combine rice flour, confectioners' sugar, potato starch, xanthan gum, baking soda, and salt in a food processor fitted with the steel blade. Blend for 5 seconds. Add butter and almond paste to the work bowl, and process until mixture resembles coarse meal.

3. Combine egg, milk, and almond extract in a small cup, and whisk well. Drizzle liquid into the work bowl, and pulse about 10 times, or until stiff dough forms. If dough is dry and doesn't come together add additional milk by 1-teaspoon amounts, until dough forms a ball.

4. Press dough into the prepared pan. Whisk egg white in a small cup and spread over dough. Pat almonds evenly onto dough.

5. Bake for 35 to 40 minutes, or until top is golden. Cool completely in the pan on a cooling rack, then cut into pieces.

VARIATION: *Substitute chocolate chips for the almonds, and omit the egg white.*

TRIASSIC TRACKS
Banana Nut Ginger Cookies (Vegan)

YIELD: 2 ½ dozen • **ACTIVE TIME:** 15 minutes
START TO FINISH: 30 minutes

INGREDIENTS:

- ½ cup chopped unsalted cashews
- ½ cup chopped blanched almonds
- 1 large ripe banana
- 1 cup all-purpose flour
- ¼ cup finely chopped crystallized ginger
- 1½ cups old-fashioned oats
- ½ cup vegetable oil
- ½ teaspoon baking soda
- ½ teaspoon ground ginger
- ¼ teaspoon salt

DIRECTIONS:

1. Preheat the oven to 350°F. Line two baking sheets with parchment paper or silicone baking mats. Place cashews and almonds on a baking sheet, and toast for 5 to 7 minutes, or until lightly browned.

2. Place banana in a mixing bowl, and mash until smooth. Stir in flour, oil, baking soda, ginger, and salt. Beat well. Stir in oats, ginger, and toasted nuts. Mix well using a sturdy spoon.

3. Drop batter by tablespoons onto the baking sheets, spacing them 2 inches apart. Bake for 10 to 12 minutes, or until edges are brown. Cool for 2 minutes on the baking sheets, and then transfer cookies to racks to cool completely.

   Note: Keep cookies in an airtight container, layered between sheets of waxed paper or parchment, at room temperature for up to 5 days. Cookies can also be frozen for up to 2 months.

MEGALODON MAPLE
Ginger Maple Cookies (Vegan)

YIELD: 3 dozen • **ACTIVE TIME:** 20 minutes
START TO FINISH: 45 minutes

INGREDIENTS:

- ¾ cup (12 tablespoons) soy margarine, softened
- 1 cup maple sugar
- ¼ cup silken tofu
- ¼ cup pure maple syrup
- 2 teaspoons baking soda
- ½ cup finely chopped crystallized ginger
- 1 teaspoon ground ginger
- ¼ teaspoon salt
- 2½ cups all-purpose flour
- ½ cup granulated sugar

DIRECTIONS:

1. Preheat the oven to 350°F. Line two baking sheets with parchment paper or silicone baking mats.

2. Combine margarine and maple sugar in a mixing bowl, and beat at low speed with an electric mixer to blend. Increase the speed to high, and beat for 3 to 4 minutes, or until light and fluffy. Beat in tofu, maple syrup, crystallized ginger, baking soda, ground ginger, and salt and beat for 1 minute. Slowly add flour to margarine mixture, and beat until soft dough forms.

3. Take scant 1-tablespoon portions of dough, and roll them into balls. Roll balls in granulated sugar. Place balls 1½ inches apart on the baking sheets.

4. Bake cookies for 12 to 15 minutes, or until top surface is cracked. Cool cookies for 2 minutes on the baking sheets, and then transfer cookies to racks to cool completely.

Note: Keep cookies in an airtight container, layered between sheets of waxed paper or parchment, at room temperature for up to 5 days. Cookies can also be frozen for up to 2 months.

MAPLE MINMI
Maple Walnut Cookies (Vegan)

YIELD: 5 dozen • **ACTIVE TIME:** 15 minutes
START TO FINISH: 2½ hours, including 2 hours to chill the dough

INGREDIENTS:

- 1 cup finely chopped walnuts
- ¾ cup pure maple syrup
- ½ cup granulated sugar
- ⅓ cup vegetable oil
- ¼ cup silken tofu
- ½ teaspoon pure vanilla extract
- 1 teaspoon baking powder
- ¼ teaspoon baking soda
- ½ teaspoon salt
- 1½ cups all-purpose flour
- 1 cup whole-wheat pastry flour

DIRECTIONS:

1. Preheat the oven to 350°F. Place walnuts on a baking sheet, and toast for 5 to 7 minutes, or until browned. Remove walnuts from the oven, and set aside. Turn off the oven. Bring maple syrup to a boil in a small saucepan over medium-high heat. Boil until reduced to ½ cup. Set aside to cool.

2. Combine reduced syrup, sugar, and oil in a mixing bowl, and beat at low speed with an electric mixer to blend. Add tofu, vanilla, baking powder, baking soda, and salt and beat for 1 minute. Slowly add all-purpose and whole-wheat flours to maple mixture, and beat until soft dough forms. Stir in walnuts.

3. Place dough on a sheet of waxed paper, and form it into a log 2½ -inches in diameter. Refrigerate dough covered in plastic wrap for 2 hours, or until firm, or up to 2 days.

4. Preheat the oven to 350°F. Line two baking sheets with parchment paper or silicone baking mats.

5. Cut chilled dough into ¼-inch slices using a sharp serrated knife, and arrange them on the baking sheets.

6. Bake cookies for 10 to 12 minutes, or until edges are brown. Cool cookies for 2 minutes on the baking sheets, and then transfer cookies to racks to cool completely.

   Note: Keep cookies in an airtight container, layered between sheets of waxed paper or parchment, at room temperature for up to 5 days. Cookies can also be frozen for up to 2 months.

MOSASAURUS MESS

Chocolate Chip Pecan Cookies (Vegan)

YIELD: 2½ dozen • **ACTIVE TIME:** 15 minutes
START TO FINISH: 40 minutes

INGREDIENTS:

- ½ cup coarsely chopped pecans
- ¼ cup soy milk
- ½ cup vegetable oil
- 1 teaspoon pure vanilla extract
- 1 cup all-purpose flour
- ½ cup whole-wheat pastry flour
- ½ cup unsweetened cocoa powder
- ¾ teaspoon baking powder
- ¼ teaspoon salt
- ¾ cup vegan dark chocolate chips
- 1½ teaspoons egg replacement powder, such as Ener-G

DIRECTIONS:

1. Preheat the oven to 350°F. Line two baking sheets with parchment paper or silicone baking mats. Place pecans on a baking sheet, and toast for 5 to 7 minutes, or until lightly browned. Set aside.

2. Mix egg replacement powder with 2 tablespoons cold water, and set aside.

3. Combine oil, egg replacement mixture, soy milk, and vanilla in a mixing bowl, and whisk well. Stir in all-purpose flour, whole-wheat flour, cocoa powder, baking powder, and salt. Beat at medium speed with an electric mixer until dough forms. Stir in dark chocolate chips and toasted pecans.

4. Drop dough by tablespoons onto the prepared baking sheets, 1½ inches apart. Bake cookies for 12 to 15 minutes, or until browned. Allow cookies to cool for 2 minutes on the baking sheets, and then transfer cookies to racks to cool completely.

Note: Keep cookies in an airtight container, layered between sheets of waxed paper or parchment, at room temperature for up to 5 days. Cookies can also be frozen for up to 2 months.

VARIATION: Substitute chopped almonds for the pecans, and add ½ teaspoons ground cinnamon.

PEPPERMINT PTERODACTYL EGGS

Peppermint Pinwheels (Gluten-Free)

YIELD: 2 dozen • **ACTIVE TIME:** 20 minutes
START TO FINISH: 3¾ hours, including 3 hours to chill the dough

INGREDIENTS:

+ 1¼ cups white rice flour
+ ¾ cup confectioners' sugar
+ ¼ cup potato starch
+ ¼ pound (1 stick) unsalted butter, thinly sliced
+ 1 teaspoon xanthan gum
+ ½ teaspoon baking soda

+ ¼ teaspoon salt
+ 1 large egg
+ 1 egg yolk
+ ½ teaspoon peppermint oil or pure peppermint extract
+ 3 to 5 drops food coloring in your favorite color!

DIRECTIONS:

1. Combine rice flour, confectioners' sugar, potato starch, xanthan gum, baking soda, and salt in a food processor fitted with the steel blade. Blend for 5 seconds. Add butter to the work bowl, and process, using on-and-off pulsing, until mixture resembles coarse meal.

2. Combine egg and egg yolk in a small cup, and whisk well. Drizzle liquid into the work bowl, and pulse about 10 times, or until stiff dough forms.

3. Remove half of dough from the food processor, and set aside. Add peppermint oil and food coloring to the food processor and process until dough is evenly colored. Wrap each dough in plastic wrap. Press dough into a pancake. Refrigerate dough for 1 hour or until firm, or up to 2 days.

4. Roll out each dough separately into a rectangle approximately ¼-inch thick. Place peppermint dough on top of the white dough, and press together around the edges. Using waxed paper or flexible cutting board underneath as a guide, roll dough into a log shape. Wrap in plastic wrap and refrigerate for 2 hours.

5. Preheat the oven to 350°F. Line two baking sheets with parchment paper or silicon baking mats.

6. Cut chilled dough into slices ¼-inch thick with a sharp serrated knife, and arrange them on the baking sheets.

7. Bake cookies for 10 to 12 minutes, or until edges are brown. Cool cookies for 2 minutes on the baking sheets, and then transfer them with a spatula to cooling racks to cool completely.

T. REX TRIPLE-THREAT

Triple Chocolate Hazelnut Cookies (Gluten-Free)

YIELD: 2½ dozen • **ACTIVE TIME:** 15 minutes
START TO FINISH: 40 minutes

INGREDIENTS:

- 1½ cups skinned hazelnuts
- ½ pound bittersweet chocolate
- 3 tablespoons unsalted butter
- 2 tablespoons brown rice flour
- 2 tablespoons unsweetened cocoa powder
- 1 tablespoon cornstarch
- ¼ teaspoon xanthan gum

- ¼ teaspoon gluten-free baking powder
- ½ cup granulated sugar
- ¼ teaspoon salt
- 2 large eggs
- 2 tablespoons Frangelico or other hazelnut-flavored liqueur
- ½ teaspoon pure vanilla extract
- 1 cup bittersweet chocolate chips

DIRECTIONS:

1. Preheat the oven to 350°F. Line two baking sheets with parchment paper or silicon baking mats. Place hazelnuts on a baking sheet, and toast for 5 to 7 minutes, or until lightly browned.

2. Break chocolate into pieces no larger than a lima bean. Either chop chocolate in a food processor fitted with a steel blade using on-and-off pulsing, or place it in a heavy re-sealable plastic bag, and smash it with the back of a heavy skillet.

3. Melt chocolate and butter in a heavy saucepan over low heat, stirring frequently until the mixture is melted and smooth. Remove the pan from the heat, and set aside for 5 to 7 minutes to cool. This can also be done in a microwave oven.

4. Combine rice flour, cocoa, cornstarch, baking powder, xanthan gum, and salt in a mixing bowl. Whisk well.

5. Combine eggs, sugar, Frangelico, and vanilla in a mixing bowl. Beat at high speed with an electric mixer for 1 minute. Beat in the cooled chocolate mixture, and then the dry ingredients. Fold in nuts and chocolate chips.

6. Drop dough by 1-tablespoon portions onto the prepared baking sheets, leaving 1½ inches of space between cookies. Bake for 10 to 12 minutes, or until tops are dry. Cool cookies on the baking sheets for 2 minutes, and then transfer to a wire rack to cool completely.

VARIATIONS: Add ½ teaspoon ground cinnamon to the dough. OR Substitute white chocolate chips for the bittersweet chocolate chips.

ICINGS

CRETACEOUS CREAM ICING

Buttercream Icing (Gluten-Free)

YIELD: 2½ cups • **ACTIVE TIME:** 15 minutes
START TO FINISH: 40 minutes

INGREDIENTS:

- 4 cups (1 pound) confectioners' sugar
- 3 tablespoons milk
- 1 teaspoon pure vanilla extract
- Food coloring (optional)
- ¼ pound (1 stick) unsalted butter, softened

DIRECTIONS:

1. Place butter, sugar, milk, and vanilla in a large mixing bowl. Beat at low speed with an electric mixer to combine. Increase the speed to high, and beat for 2 minutes, or until light and fluffy.

2. If tinting icing, transfer it to small cups and add food coloring, a few drops at a time, until desired color is reached. Stir well before adding additional coloring.

   Note: The icing can be kept refrigerated in an airtight container for up to five days. Bring it to room temperature before using.

HOW TO USE:

Buttercream is a wonderful icing to use to make rosettes or other complex decorations with a pastry bag. Add additional confectioners' sugar in 1-tablespoon increments if not stiff enough.

43

DINO DIG-IN GLAZE
Confectioner's Sugar Glaze (Gluten-Free)

YIELD: 1½ cups • **ACTIVE TIME:** 5 minutes
START TO FINISH: 5 minutes

INGREDIENTS:

+ 4 cups (1 pound) confectioners' sugar
+ 4-5 tablespoons water
+ 1 teaspoon clear vanilla extract
+ Food coloring (optional)

DIRECTIONS:

1. Combine confectioners' sugar, 4 tablespoons water, and vanilla in a mixing bowl. Stir until smooth, adding additional water if too thick.

2. If tinting the glaze, transfer it to small cups and add food coloring, a few drops at a time, until desired color is reached. Stir well before adding additional coloring.

Note: The glaze can be kept at room temperature in an airtight container, with a sheet of plastic wrap pressed directly into the surface, for up 6 hours. Beat it again lightly to emulsify before using.

HOW TO USE:

This glaze is not strong enough to hold large candies, but it can be used as "glue" for small items like jimmies. One way to use it is to spread the white glaze on cooled cookies and allow it to dry hard. Then mix 1 teaspoon of water into ¼ cup of the glaze, and tint it with food coloring. Crumple up a sheet of waxed paper and dip it into the tinted glaze; then dab the cookies and you'll have a marbled effect.

ROYAL RAPTOR ICING

Royal Icing (Gluten-Free)

YIELD: 3½ cups • **ACTIVE TIME:** 5 minutes
START TO FINISH: 12 minutes

INGREDIENTS:

+ ½ teaspoon cream of tartar
+ ¼ teaspoon salt
+ 3 large egg whites, at room temperature
+ 4 cups (1 pound) confectioners' sugar
+ ½ teaspoon pure vanilla extract
+ Food coloring (optional)

DIRECTIONS:

1. Place egg whites in a grease-free mixing bowl and beat at medium speed with an electric mixer until frothy. Add the cream of tartar and salt, raise the speed to high, and beat until soft peaks form.

2. Add sugar and beat at low speed to moisten. Raise the speed to high, and beat for 5 to 7 minutes, or until mixture is glossy and stiff peaks form. Beat in vanilla.

3. If tinting icing, transfer it to small cups and add food coloring, a few drops at a time, until desired consistency is reached. Stir well before adding additional coloring.

   Note: The icing can be kept at room temperature in an airtight container for up to 2 days. Beat it again lightly to emulsify before using.

HOW TO USE:

Icing of this consistency is perfect to pipe decorations onto cooled cookies, and you can also use it as the "glue" to affix candies. If you want to paint the cookies with frosting, thin the icing with milk in 1-teaspoon amounts until the proper consistency is reached.

BONUS!
T. Rex True or False Quiz

1. **T/F** Leaves and grass were T. rex's favorite foods.
2. **T/F** It could bite down harder than a great white shark.
3. **T/F** T. rex eggs were green and shaped like chicken eggs.
4. **T/F** T. rex ate both flesh and bone.
5. **T/F** The Spinosaurus was a relative of T. rex.
6. **T/F** It could weigh more than an African Elephant.
7. **T/F** T. rex fossils have been found in Canada.
8. **T/F** T. rex lived during the Jurassic period, like the movie!
9. **T/F** Tyrannosaurus rex means "King of the Dinosaurs."
10. **T/F** T. rex can run faster than the average human.

From *The T. Rex Handbook* by Brian Switek

ANSWERS: 1-F; 2-T; 3-F; 4-T; 5-F; 6-T; 7-T; 8-F; 9-F; 10-T

ABOUT APPLESAUCE PRESS BOOK PUBLISHERS

Good ideas ripen with time. From seed to harvest, Applesauce Press creates books with beautiful designs, creative formats, and kid-friendly information. Like our parent company, Cider Mill Press Book Publishers, our press bears fruit twice a year, publishing a new crop of titles each spring and fall.

"Where Good Books Are Ready for Press"

Visit us on the web at
www.cidermillpress.com
or write to us at
12 Spring St., PO Box 454
Kennebunkport, Maine 04046